Their Sobering Suicides

poems by

Lisa Richards

Finishing Line Press
Georgetown, Kentucky

Their Sobering Suicides

Publisher: Leah Maines

Editor: Christen Kincaid

Cover Art: Lisa RIchards

Author Photo: Mark DeJohn, www.dejohnphotography.com

Cover Design: Elizabeth Maines

Printed in the USA on acid-free paper.
Order online: www.finishinglinepress.com
            also available on amazon.com

Author inquiries and mail orders:
Finishing Line Press
P. O. Box 1626
Georgetown, Kentucky 40324
U. S. A.

Table of Contents

Ever After... 1

For Ken: Detroit Street.. 2

Speaking of My Daughter... 4

Victory Cake 7

In That Moment.. 8

Wake Up 10

Free at Last.. 12

Please Save... 15

Fresh Flowers 18

Tour Guide 19

1955.. 21

For Ken Sann   *and*   *Mallory Erin Richards*
11/29/67—7/28/14   *8/8/92—1/4/11*

I am not resigned to the shutting away of
loving hearts in the hard ground.

~Edna St. Vincent Millay, *Dirge Without Music*

Ever After

In the ever after
dust settles over
all   is itself leveled   we
fight this knowing with velocity
diseased thinking   the ego   the loudest
culprit it destroys
hope   we are tricksters.

I was born knowing
more than a kid should or wants to.
Orange skies   broken bones of a mother
a girl herself   the once calm air
polluted with sirens
a dismembered door is this why
my walls were made so
thin? Herded into an offender's vehicle
for fifteen years like a calf on
her last   hopes no more

Yet miracle, I held love   they
were not supposed to leave: Daughter. Brother.
how could they/I do
this   they are teachers of dust
and hope   I
walk the earth stunned dead hopeful
Can I translate what happened and
will you listen.
Can I be dust and here and walk
among you and will you know.

The song the sun the ocean roar
The relative calm of the protected fetus
The miracles the perfect beauty on
the other side
the things that could go wrong.

For Ken : Detroit Street

Through day's flame I arrive,
In hot chrome and restlessness
At our beginnings again: Detroit Street
Its' brisket smells, angry boy alleys
Where the silent sisters stood, and hearts ticked
Like bombs, beyond the parochial school

Our mother's kingdom was a duplex of depravity
Where people were cruel or to be pitied.
Where shame was the one paddle—
Walls of obscurity walls of steel
She was a funhouse mirror we lived
Under her heel, rising for painkillers
In the slow death of childhood.

Youngest brother, you did what you could—
Cuffed to cruelty, aping fatherhood
From a man you barely knew:
Nights, through the grates of my floor heater,
He wept like a kicked newborn
In her shadow

                             *

Decades, you and I engineered true north roads
From which to be reborn: Marriages. Children. Honest Work.
You left off the shoulders
I omitted crown and swale, rainwater everywhere
We ignored signals, drove drunk on our own debasement
No parkland regional landscape could endure,

Paths that led everywhere but back to ourselves, so that
For all the time capsules we concealed,
The miles we logged across tenacious hearts' terrain,
And the harm we left for others to inflict,
We never vacated.

Speaking of My Daughter

You would rather throw stones at a mirror?
I am your mirror and here are the stones
~Rumi

Tiny prayer,
whose innocence could crush hate and greed before she went—
in this life, they look at lambs for food.

Her eyes were a prism through which my colors
Sparkled. Separated.
Through which even the black became oddly beautiful.
Then a four-year crescendo:
Broken, with perilous adhesives,
She boarded an expedited train.
I could only dream of keeping up in the end.

Now, in her violent absence,
(an irrepressible statement about our times
voiced from eternal silence),
There is but one dream only:
of lambs overtaking the earth.
Of the cold becoming compassionate.
Of the mentally ill cornering their shame
and disowning their inheritance.

It is a dream
of awakening the white collar criminals
for whom integrity
has become a yawned-over bullet point
at a dinner meeting with colleagues—
until it's you who gets caught
doing what's morally unthinkable.
Unless it's *your* hands
that now wear the indelible blood
of a child on a fast moving train
regardless of who smiles back
or flies you to the Amazon
or publishes your research.

Because when looking upon human decency
as a politically-charged commodity,
when there are bills to pay
and reputations to protect,
and mirrors you just won't face
if the view doesn't flatter—
the loss of a young life
is not the only thing that you will mourn.

And mourning, you just may
blame the horn blower
for the emperor's lack of clothing
so that neither emperor nor his men
need find in their mirror
the next-to-last folded domino
in the death of a child
in the life of an American family—
But, drunk on power,
they would not listen.
And so this train with her on it
quickened its' speed to the dreaded destination.

It is a dream
of understanding
that every breath of every life is a ripple.
That the ripple effects the all.
That the all writes history.
That the all creates the one.

The ripple is ongoing.
It did not begin with my child
and it does not end with me.

The stones you've tossed
out onto the middle of the lake
have left your hands.

And beyond my last breath,
you will remember
that one and all, we are the lake.

We are the stone. The ripple too, is us.
And everything we have done to one another
or ourselves, without wisdom
or love, or compassion, or integrity,
will become the supple earth
through which we, the whole of humanity,
will fall to our ultimate destruction.

And my daughter's life will have meant that much.

Victory Cake

Your daughters ate Quinceanera cake together. Dulce de leche, three layers,
Your husband drove dutifully to the bakery. Looks of a beauty queen,

You knew how to bend the wind in your favor. But guests return
Home, and narcissism leaves puncture wounds from the sharpest teeth

Dripping venom from the walls of the bedroom at night. Up and
Down the spine. Hugging respectable roads to the bakery, even,

If you let it. On the telephone to his family,
Building your case: Hate *him*. Hate *him and not me.*

A village girl must never show her history
Of leather belts glistening for a loved one's pleasure. Lineages

Of brutality are handed down every day. Cross dinner tables and countries,
Tiptoe through *No War* zones. Enter hospitals. But this one, you handed

To me. To the friends and co-workers
Who photographed your leather belt collection

For a courtroom. Every cake you now taste will be layered
In his blood. You have been permanently crowned with his agony.

In That Moment

When I woke to the news, a pared-down e-mail
Sent from a boat on a lake in Italy,

Of the fact (there could be just one)—
That you did it, that the thing we feared for

Years, had come to pass—that twice now, in the
Life of an American family, in under four years, a half-

Century of pillaged hope had nestled in our bones
And grafted its collective scar onto the human family—

When the sequence of contributing factors
Invaded my consciousness, like tar flushed into breathing spaces:

Genetics, trauma, maniacal efforts to disavow a shattered
Will and, the purging of your spirit by another—

When I knew in an instant, that my training had gone out the
Window, with poorly delivered expressions of concern, with

Cars full of groceries, and a man-bracelet carved with your
Child's name, for a desolate Father's Day, made more desolate

By my failure to act, and a George Foreman indoor grill,
Once, and money, even, but you needed intervention

You needed *my* unshattered will, *my* refusal to go
Away, even as you'd send me packing *I don't want to talk about it*—

When I returned, at the moment of my knowing of your death,
To truths rooted in me like starved trees

Or the impetuous silence of muffled songbirds,
When I stared down my own jail of illusions, and my

Hijacking toward glitter, I
Understood in that moment the story you were

Here to teach us all—the same one your leaving
Now emblazons on our consciousness—

That the boat saves or capsizes the whole of us. That what
Life ignores, death will surely scream. That some

Doors are meant to close in broad daylight,
While others prop open only to the sun.

Wake Up

> *Scholarly knowledge is a vertigo,*
> *an exhausted famousness.*
> *Listening is better.*
>
> ~*Rumi*

Big things flatten into scrapbooks.
Where else can grey turn to gold

Or the tunnel people admit their openings.
By daylight, ghosts nibble at the edges of my life

At night, the dead ones hover around my throat
In what I am quite sure is meant to be an intimate display of their love.

Look, my daughter says in one recent dream,
As cotton ball clouds fill a theater light-infused cornflower blue sky

Like an endless backdrop, *You were right*:
I needed drug rehab. It could've saved my life.

Prevailing Afterlife research suggests this was not a dream,
That she was *visiting* me, and that her revelation was a *gift*.

I awaken to her absence, with a Pavlovian response
To the sounds of children outside my window

And my life shrink-wrapped to a baby's blanket.

*

I was a weak, indulgent, people-pleasing, shame-stuffed mother
But when ravens piled at my throat

And a death rattle ringing in my ears, came for my child,
My daughter's doctor turned up the noise,

And went home.
So I guess this would be an emergency.

Detritus addling the edges of her brilliance.
You know what Gandhi said about science without humanity.

*

Muzzle me with your shame, bandage me in your lies
Bring me my robes of mourning and my broken milk

And I will eat your self-serving disreputable stories
like toast for a ghost.

Free At Last

From early childhood, the bars were in your mind:
captivity by a mother's cruelty

lies eating into your soul,
unsuspecting host.

No one knew
you were half-gone by high school.

So loving, so capable you seemed.
Elated on a motorcycle.

Ably defiant for a while.
Eventually, this:

Deliriously happy with your child
who you swore you'd never leave.

But by birth, she also bound you
to the weapon of your annihilation.

I should have known, so clear is it now
that you and I

were twins in this fundamental way:
aching to please, to give without thought

of self. So foolish, so finally empty,
doors relaxed to the soul murderers,

each one a handshake to a mother's cruelty.
So that with decent minds

but the compulsive blindness of the traumatized,
we sought hatred's dirge

and the gutted feeling from other peoples' greed.
Over and again, you gave to me.

Held my hand, as my daughter
lay folded on a metal table. Mirror to my ignorance.

How you fed me the next day, traipsed with me
to the cemetery. The police department.

Duties of the destitute. Things love does without thought.
Yet, soon thereafter, the gift in need of repayment,

I allowed you to push me away
when the words *Please help me* rested like cyanide on your tongue.

*

She took a hammer to your motorcycle
and a boulder to your rear car
window

in the rain.
And now, as I lie folded in my own way,

with your absence,
you tenderly guide me home.

We are the witnesses
who live to tell the story,

a story your own child
translates

by flashlight within her soul.
A soul that would be ravaged by a mother's cruelty.

Except that you were here.

Please Save

But how will we put the birds back up in the sky, Momma?
You asked me, at age five. I was trying
to rescue two hurt doves.
And, I cannot remember
what distressed them,
or if they survived. What stays is your conviction
that they needed to fly.   That it was up to me.

I lifted a young starling from our cat's mouth, once,
Its' toothpick legs dangling through her teeth.
And tossed a ball toward a crow honed in
on a squirrel deep up into the elm tree.
I had meddled with nature and I knew it. But the squirrel lived
and our road trip happened, then, without incident.

There was Rainbow the dog
vocal chords clipped by heathens before she fell
—or was she tossed?—from a pick-up truck's basin.
Eyewitness News sent folks clamoring
to make her a back-yard guard dog. But I promised you, *No*—

We fattened her on ground turkey and raw eggs
while, singing, you clung to my pajama bottoms in the kitchen.
She made Hospice visits
and swam in a lake, before arthritis
crippled her, and cancer, and she went.

But six years later, *you*, my only child,
my life, my elm, my sky—*you* fell from on high.
Chased by fiends I'd forgotten
And entered the belly of the beast.

There were doctors and cops—
Emergency meetings and near-constant anxiety: Mine.
Suicide contracts and runaways: Yours.
Great-Uncle Hal, hunched over on the Venice Boardwalk
while Uncle Ken, with a broken foot
hobbled through alleys, speaking your name.

I asked myself: If I found you there, what would I say?
Would you speak to me?
You were halfway gone already, but I bargained with God:
What's one more dove?

There were airplanes and schools for the ill
and frozen dinner holidays reading your letters.
Inked scavenger hunts for hope
That now crumble in my hands,
your DNA on their fibers more alive now than you will ever be.

There were phone calls and care-packages
And your Uncle Ken sobbing in a rental car
over your MDMA and meth psychosis

There were bullies, and pot stirrers, and friends with love soup.
there were wise good therapists
and advice columnists with diplomas
there were bad mother morality plays
which cast me as a shrew, when in fact,
I was just dangerously blind and pitiful.

Finally, a sad *pas de deux*
The matador and the doomed bull
The closing of the cat's mouth where I could no longer reach.
The slow disintegration of a paper mother in the stands.
The deception by two ivory tower showmen.
banking on you as a junket
As if what we see, we do not change, in the seeing.
As if radical suffering were not a clarion call to compassionate action.
As if, when tethered to our capes and our gutlessness,
We are truly surprised when the brute life drains and the arena empties

Fresh Flowers

From a prom date in high school.
For the wrist corsage worn therein.
From a friend in college for treating her to a Kenny Rankin concert.
Gardenia lei gifted for my grad school commencement.
From several boyfriends.
From my future husband for the first time we made love.
On my wedding day.
From a client for helping her immensely, she said.
For the birth of my daughter.
From a friend comforting me when my marriage ended.
To my daughter because I loved her.
To my daughter to give her something beautiful to look at in her room.
To my daughter when we strolled the Farmers Market at Wilson Park
one crowded Saturday.
To my daughter for her performances in several summer, two winter
drama camps.
To my daughter for her sixteenth birthday spent in a Utah treatment
facility.
To my daughter because I loved her more.
For my daughter's final boxed-up send-off in a bone ceremony.
And each year, onto the marble wall the day my child nosedived into
the cold black soup of eternity.

Tour Guide

From the island of PTSD, the past hovers at your shores.
Your brother's eyes lit, your daughter's laughter
Before it was felled—
All drowned now in the white foam viscera spun out
Like eternity's last wash in the twinkling sun.
What you've cherished, and lost. Family. Your
Sanity. And holidays
Adrift now, on a sea of memory,
Are part of an aged, grand flotilla that no longer docks for you.

From eyes that can't stop looking, you turn
To still life in a casket, your young daughter's face
Painted like a streetwalker
After three failed efforts to give back her damaged life.

And your brother's chilled lineament and moist eyelashes
Where he lay on a gurney—
Two years, he dreamt his escape.
Months in the planning stages.

How your loved ones dissolved like foam. How they dissolved—
And willed you this knapsack of their suffering

                        *

Even a leaf from a Portia tree
Can startle,
Showing what you've become.
A still swaying voyage of gust and stillness.

And when the mirage appears,
The one about your life
Being salvageable, you rock fetal
On a hammock of a different knowing.
Yet you adapt.
Clean up fair,
And step onto the mainland,
Toting cheer and helpfulness.
Honest days' work. Thirst
For light companionship quenched in jaunts
Before the longed-for return to your final stopover:
The place from which it is but a brief footpath
To the cyan waters of grief and honesty.

1955

I
1955.
From the moon's hip, a black egg emerges
Onto the scene: A small tract home
In California. People trying to love and be loved. Except that,
Neither knows/believes that love was in their origins.
Strains follow this misunderstanding.
Another egg, then. Black? I can't be sure. What I do know
Is that a violent riot happened, several maybe, and the police
Came, and the home broke apart like a suicide bomber.
—Some things were never meant to mingle.
Was the black really me? A soul that knows
No love in its origins has black waters running through its veins.

II
My mother works for the Diner's Club.
We moisten sponges to put blue chip stamps
Into her book. *Fill the pages*, she says.
Fill the pages, and we can buy something.
I enter another abyss now, where I court the world
Of stories. Stories to keep myself sane.
My mother loves me. My father doesn't mean to terrify me.
Buy things, sit next to your father in the speeding car,
My mother says. In my stories, I lift her up high
Into the clouds where she can do no wrong.
Night stars drift downward in a gaggle
Blinding me from the ruinous years.
I tell myself that this must be my mother.
You'll probably just grow up and have children, she says.

III

A new father. Two bright, golden, adorable eggs.
My mother's contentment subdues her mood swings:
Jugular rage or suffocating intrusion.
My two golden eggs
(Well, in my stories, they are mine)
Teach me there are reasons and ways to love.
That the black and the stars are more, for each other.
My new father shows me how to twirl
Spaghetti against a spoon.
On a family camping trip,
We slip on our tennis shoes without laces
And wade into the river with our curly-haired mutt.
The sharp rocks across the river bed
Are my life. The river runs fast like hope. Cold. Fresh. Pure.
We eat pancakes from a Coleman.
This is after we steer the boats at McArthur Park
And my mother makes Farmers' Chop Suey in the summertime.
This is years before we cross the Mexican border,
Wearing sombreros on a painted burro
And skip across the pebbly streets,
Singing (badly) *La Cucaracha*
And my mother makes my new father weep for not making more money
And he touches me where no father old or new should ever go.

IV
I smell freedom at the Teenage Fair at the Hollywood Palladium.
My soul begins to undergo a transfusion
While my mother seethes with cruelty
Over what was stolen from her: Cold. Fresh. Pure.
My first father nods at my soul work, then issues me
A citation for my wrongdoings. Which means
Not holding his soul house together.
My new father leaves his life at the hospital
Weeks before I graduate high school
My mother and our family blow apart
And I run for my life
Not knowing where or how to go.
By now, however, I have learned how to front.
And my banished love for two underage brothers
—One courts, one dodges the blackness—
Becomes a longstanding ache.
Elsewhere, I grieve for the far-off, lamp-lit windows
That do not light for me. *Outsider. Interloper.*
And this makes me compassionate
And yet, walking among the stones without your shoes
Will get you everywhere but where you need to go.

V
I chisel my mind. I train
And polish and discipline it
So that my mind can be me.
A me that has no closures
A me that is hollow of rage or indignance
Like a thoroughfare
With the mindlessness of thieves who rob themselves
A me that cannot be cited or fondled or hated
For breathing life (what I thought
Was life), unto itself.
A me with boundaries of salt.
When the world splits apart
And pieces of you settle
Along the river bed
 Like sharp rocks or sediment,
You thirst for water not knowing
That water is where you are.
I lift the people in my life high up into the air
Where they can do no wrong.
Meanwhile, at the river's bottom, I roll in tight
And wait for the swift clean water
To pour over me as it passes.
Wait, I say. *Please wait.*

VI

Within a marriage, I am blessed with a daughter,
And the marriage does not last,
But the daughter remains for years,
Happy. Robust. Playful.
We ride the Coast Starlight in a sleeping car
To San Luis Obispo
Where, at the Childrens' Museum,
She slips on a silver ballerina costume
And, barefooted, sings atop a piano.
We laugh when grazing horses at Cal Poly
Slobber across our palms for sugar cubes.
My daughter embroiders a pillow for our dying cat
And we pick apples at the orchards at Oak Glen, once.
I lift her high up into the air
And everyone says, *Your daughter is*
Loving kind sensitive sweet
But I think to myself, that is also
How you can get yourself to the bottom of the river

VII

At sixteen, my daughter smells freedom
On the Venice Boardwalk
Trading both sex for crack
And a mother who
Does not understand how to live with closures,
For stories.
There is pain in my daughter's eyes
From being banished at school
And wildness
From taking in bits of shrapnel
That have migrated slowly
From the far side of me.
Not everything surfaces or exits when it should.

VIII
And my daughter builds a thoroughfare.
And my youngest brother
Who's over forty, now,
Reaches for my daughter
With love so pure and he
Tries to bring her back
(Even as *he* also
Needs to be brought back)
We try to bring her
Back   home, and a therapist
With closures everywhere, like my mother,
Says to me when I protest,
Because her methods appear to bring
Old dangers for my child, she says,
Don't be such an interloper.
And in January of her eighteenth year of life,
My daughter then says to me one evening
I've gotta go—
But I do not see that she is talking about
Her life.
From my openings to a therapist's closures,
I have chiseled and trained myself to stay out of the way.
My daughter ends her life the next day.

IX
And my youngest brother,
Having had his own soul gutted
Like a fish left flapping to its slow-motion death
On the riverbank, for years—
He ends his life too, at forty-six,
Within three-point-five years' time
Of my daughter's leaving.
With unspeakable pain
With the loneliness of air
My loved ones removed their shoes
Excised the black waters
Drained the rivers snipped
Down all the lifted up people
Blinded the stars said Fuck Yes we
Are sick the world is sick
Every suicide tells a story
Will you listen
Will you listen
Will you listen

Lisa Richards earned her B.A. in English and Creative Writing from U.C.L.A., and her M.S.W. from U.S.C. She is a Board Certified Diplomat in Clinical Social Work, and has maintained a consulting practice in Southern California for over thirty years. She is published in her field and has presented at numerous conferences.

Lisa received an Honorable Mention from the Academy of American Poets. She recently won residencies from Turkey Land Cove Foundation, Hypatia-in-the-Woods, and University of Washington's Helen Riaboff Whiteley Center.

In 2012, Lisa co-authored *Dear Mallory: Letters To a Teenage Girl Who Killed Herself* (New Middle Press) following the 2011 suicide of her only child. *Dear Mallory* received an Honorable Mention in the Eric Hoffer Book Awards, and was called "hauntingly candid" by The Journal of the American Academy of Child and Adolescent Psychiatry. *Dear Mallory* has been added to the recommended reading list of the American Association of Suicidology, and is being used as a suicide prevention tool in schools and psychotherapy offices. *Dear Mallory* is also a resource for survivors of suicide loss. For more information, please go to www.dearmalloryletters.com

www.ingramcontent.com/pod-product-compliance
Lightning Source LLC
LaVergne TN
LVHW041329080426
835513LV00008B/646